homest filip
cooking

Norma Olizon-Chikiamco

PERIPLUS

Basic Filipino Ingredients

Beancurd is known as *tokwa* in Tagalog. Rich in protein, it can be steamed or deep-fried, pickled or fermented. Soft white *tokwa* is steamed or added to soups; hard squares of *tokwa* are deep-fried; small cubes of dried beancurd are added to slow-cooked dishes. Red or white fermented *tokwa*, sold in jars, is used as a seasoning.

Calamansi is a small walnut-sized green to yellow-green fruit with an aromatic citrus flavor. *Calamansi* makes a delicious fresh juice and adds its lively accent to many foods, from noodles to desserts.

Capsicum, also known as bell peppers, are often used in fresh salads and Spanish-style dishes or stews.

Cornflour or cornstarch is a fine white powder often used as a thickening agent. It does not add much fat or change the flavor of a dish.

Eggplant (aubergines), known as *talong* in Tagalog, is of the slender purple-skinned variety. *Talong* is usually grilled over the stove before being chopped and made into a salad; or stuffed (*Rellenong Talong*); or sautéed in a vegetable dish like Pinakbet.

Kangkong is a deep-green aquatic plant with heart-shaped leaves, popular throughout Southeast Asia. Also known as water convolvulus and sometimes water spinach or swamp cabbage, it is full of nutrition and possesses an excellent flavor. It is sautéed with garlic or mixed into *sinigang*.

Pan de sal is the national bread of the Philippines, which is shaped like a

Fresg egg noodles

Glass noodles

Dried egg noodles

Rice vermicelli

Noodles can be made from rice or wheat flour or mung beans. Among Filipinos, the most popular varieties are *kanton*, thick, round, yellow fresh egg noodles; *bihon*, dried rice vermicelli; and *sotanghon*, transparent mung-bean noodles, also known as cellophane or glass noodles. *Pancit* is a generic term used to refer to a noodle dish.

Soy sauce is probably the best known Asian seasoning agent, brewed from soybeans, wheat and salt. It is available in several forms—light, dark and sweet soy sauce. Light or "regular" soy sauce is used in this book. It is saltier, less malty in flavor and thinner than black soy sauce. Soy sauce is available in bottles—in supermarkets and provision shops.

Dark Soy Sauce   Light Soy Sauce

bun. Substitute any bread of your choice.

Patis is a thin fish sauce made from boiled, salted and fermented fish or shrimp. It is used to flavor many dishes. An essential item to have on hand but, if unavailable, substitute Thai *nam pla* or Vietnamese *nuoc mam*.

Red egg (*itlog na maalat*), or salted duck egg, is a savory condiment or side dish that has been boiled, stored in brine and dyed red.

Saba is a type of cooking banana, very similar to plantain bananas. It is light to bright yellow in color, with a yellowish-black peel.

Singkamas also known as *Jicama*, or yam bean, is a crunchy white turnip which is sautéed as a filling for Lumpia.

Spring onion is also known as scallion. This popular green young onion is used as a flavoring in soups and a garnish on meat dishes.

Spring roll wrapper is a thin crêpe made from a batter of rice flour, water and salt. The *lumpia* wrapper is steamed and dried in the sun, then used to wrap a variety of spring rolls. The rice wrapper must be moistened with a wet cloth before using, for greater flexibility.

Ubod is the white pith of the heart of a palm (coconut or *buri*). It is blanched and served as a fresh salad or cooked as a vegetable in the traditional Lumpiang Ubod.

Vinegar, also known as *suka* or native vinegar, comes in black, red and white hues. It is made from *nipa* palm, coconut, *kaong* or sago palm, as well as from sugar cane. White vinegar can be used for the recipes in this book.

Eggplant Relish

6 medium eggplants
(aubergines)
Juice of 3 *calamansi*
3 cloves garlic, crushed
60 ml ($^1/_4$ cup) vinegar
Salt
Freshly ground black
pepper
Diced tomato, to garnish
(optional)
Chopped spring onions,
to garnish (optional)

1 Grill eggplants over medium heat until tender, about 15 minutes. Peel and, using the back of a spoon or a fork, mash eggplants finely. Sprinkle with *calamansi* juice and let stand a few minutes.

2 In a small bowl, combine garlic and vinegar. Pour over the mashed eggplants. Season with salt and pepper. Mix well. If desired, garnish with tomato and spring onions for added color.

3 Serve as relish for Pochero, and fried or steamed fish.

Makes about 1$^1/_2$ cups
Preparation time: **10–15 mins**
Cooking time: **15 mins**

Vinegar-Soy Calamansi Dip

125 ml ($^1/_2$ cup) soy sauce
60 ml ($^1/_4$ cup) vinegar
60 ml ($^1/_4$ cup) *calamansi* juice
3–4 cloves garlic, crushed
1 tablespoon sugar
4–5 spring onions,
chopped
60 ml ($^1/_4$ cup) water
Dash of pepper or
chopped finger chilies
for extra heat

1 Combine all the ingredients in a bowl. Set aside for several minutes to allow the flavors to blend.

2 Serve as a dip for grilled or fried fish, grilled squid or grilled pork.

Makes about 1 cup
Preparation time: **5 mins**

Garlic Mayonnaise Dip

125 ml ($^1/_2$ cup) mayonnaise
Cloves of $^1/_2$ head garlic,
finely crushed
1 teaspoon white sugar
1 teaspoon liquid season-
ing (such as Knorr or
Maggi)
Salt and pepper to taste

1 In a bowl, mix all ingredients together until smooth.

2 Serve as a dip with Calamares.

Makes about $^1/_2$ cup
Preparation time: **5 mins**

Green Mango and Tomato Relish

1 green (unripe) mango
3 small red tomatoes
1 small onion
1 tablespoon white refined sugar (or more to taste)
2 tablespoons *patis* (fish sauce)
1 tablespoon *calamansi* juice

1 Peel mango and cut the flesh into 1-cm ($1/2$-in) cubes; discard the mango seed. Slice the tomatoes and onion into similar sized pieces; combine with mango.
2 In a small bowl, blend together sugar, *patis* and *calamansi* juice. Pour over mango, tomato and onion mixture. Stir to mix well. Let stand a few minutes.
3 Serve as relish for Tapa, Tocino, Adobo and fried fish.

Serves 4
Preparation time: **10 mins**

Acharang Labanos (Pickled Radish and Carrots)

3 medium white radishes, about 400 g (13 oz), peeled and cut in paper-thin round slices, mashed with $1/2$–$3/4$ cup coarse salt and set aside several hours
300 g ($1 1/2$ cups) white refined sugar
250 ml (1 cup) white or cane vinegar
2 medium carrots, peeled and cut in paper-thin round slices

1 Rinse radish slices in water, making sure to remove all the salt. Squeeze out all the water. Set aside.
2 Combine sugar and vinegar in a saucepan and stir to combine. Simmer over low heat until mixture becomes clear, about 3 minutes. Add the radish and carrots. Simmer for about 5 minutes.
3 Remove from heat and, using a slotted spoon, transfer radish and carrots to a clean glass bowl. Pour in a little of the vinegar-sugar syrup. Let cool, then store in a covered container. Keep in the refrigerator and use as relish for fried fish, barbecues and fried chicken.

Makes 2 cups
Preparation time: **20 mins + several hours soaking**
Cooking time: **10 mins**

Sour Cream-Mayonnaise Dip

125 ml ($1/2$ cup) mayonnaise
125 ml ($1/2$ cup) sour cream
3–4 cloves garlic, finely crushed
1 teaspoon *adobo* seasoning (optional)
Salt and pepper to taste

1 In a bowl, mix mayonnaise and sour cream until smooth. Add garlic and adobo seasoning, if desired. Season with salt and pepper to taste.
2 Serve as a dip with Kangkong Fritters.

Makes about 1 cup
Preparation time: **5 mins**

Gambas (Spicy Prawns)

1 kg (2 lb) medium prawns, peeled (heads, tails and shells discarded)
Juice of 3–4 *calamansi*
60 ml (¹/₄ cup) olive oil
Cloves of 1 whole head of garlic, peeled and crushed
Dash Tabasco (or other hot pepper sauce)
Salt and pepper to taste
Parsley, to garnish (optional)
Sliced green chili, to garnish (optional)

1 Marinate peeled prawns in *calamansi* juice for about 30 minutes.
2 Heat oil in a frying pan or wok and sauté garlic until almost brown. Add prawns and stir-fry until fully cooked, about 2 to 3 minutes. Do not overcook.
3 Season with hot pepper sauce and salt and pepper to taste. Transfer prawns to a serving dish together with the garlic. If desired, garnish with parsley and chili. Serve as an appetizer, as a first course or as *pulutan* with drinks.

Serves 6
Preparation time: 20 mins + 30 mins marinating
Cooking time: 5 mins

Kangkong Fritters

Kangkong, or water convolvulus, is a lowly swamp cabbage that grows wild in the fields. Here, it is elevated to an attractive appetizer, coated in batter and fried to a crisp. A good substitute for *kangkong* is spinach.

1 bunch *kangkong*, about 200 g (7 oz)
750 ml (3 cups) iced water
125 g (1 cup) plain (all-purpose) flour
125 g (1 cup) cornflour
1 egg
500 ml (2 cups) water for the batter
500 ml (2 cups) oil
Salt and pepper to taste

Serves 6
Preparation time: **30 mins**
Cooking time: **30 mins**

1 Wash *kangkong* and separate the leaves from the stalks. Cut the stalks into 2-cm (1-in) pieces. Soak leaves and stalks in iced water for 30 minutes.

2 In a deep bowl, make a dipping batter by combining flour, cornflour, egg and the 500 ml (2 cups) water. Mix until batter is smooth.

3 Drain *kangkong* leaves and stalks and pat dry with paper towels. Heat cooking oil in a wok. Dip leaves and stalks in the batter and fry four or five pieces at a time in the hot oil, turning once. Cook until the leaves firm up and become crisp, about 1 to 2 minutes on each side. Remove from oil and drain on paper towels. Serve with Sour Cream-Mayonnaise Dip (see page 5).

Tokwa't Baboy (Tau Kwa and Pork in Vinaigrette)

1–2 blocks, about 500 g (1 lb) *tau kwa*
60 ml (¹/₄ cup) oil
1 small onion, chopped
125 ml (¹/₂ cup) vinegar
60 ml (¹/₄ cup) soy sauce
250 g (8 oz) pork head, simmered 1 hour, cubed (optional)
500 g (1 lb) pork shoulder, simmered 30 mins, cubed
Chopped spring onions, to garnish (optional)

1 Pat the *tau kwa* dry if it is moist, then cut into cubes. Heat oil and fry the *tau kwa* pieces in batches until they turn brown, about 2 to 3 minutes each side. Remove from heat and drain on paper towels.
2 In a mixing bowl, mix together onion, vinegar and soy sauce. Taste mixture; if it's too sour, add a little water. Let stand a few minutes for flavors to blend.
3 In a large bowl combine the diced pork head, pork shoulder and *tau kwa*.
4 Pour the soy sauce/vinegar onion mixture over the diced meats and *tau kwa*. Stir to mix. If desired, garnish with spring onions.
5 Serve as a side dish with noodles or other dishes.

Serves 6–8
Preparation time: **30 mins (1 hour if using pork head)**
Cooking time: **15–20 mins**

Calamares (Calamari with Lime)

Often served in bars and bistros as an accompaniment to drinks, Calamares is a dish of Spanish origin adapted by Filipinos and localised with the use of *calamansi*.

1 kg (2 lb) medium squid, cleaned (head, ink sacs and tentacles discarded), outer purple skin peeled off (do not cut squid open)
Juice of 3–4 *calamansi*
2 egg whites
125 g (1 cup) plain (all-purpose) flour
250 ml (1 cup) oil
Salt and pepper to taste
Lettuce (optional)

1 Slice squid into 1-cm ($^1/_2$-in) rings. Marinate in *calamansi* juice for about 30 minutes.

2 Dip squid rings in egg whites, then dredge in flour.

3 Heat oil in a wok and fry squid rings in hot oil a few pieces at a time until they turn golden yellow, about 1 minute. Do not overcook as this will make the squid tough. Remove squid rings from the wok and drain on paper towels. Season with salt and pepper.

4 If desired, place on a bed of lettuce. Serve with Garlic Mayonnaise Dip (see page 4) as an appetizer or as a *pulutan* with drinks.

Serves 6
Preparation time: **15 + 30 mins marinating**
Cooking time: **15–20 mins**

Nilagang Manok (Chicken and Vegetable Soup)

1 kg (2 lb) whole chicken, cut into serving pieces
1 medium onion, sliced lengthwise
2 liters (8 cups) water
1–2 medium potatoes, peeled and quartered
4 *saba* (plantain) bananas, each sliced into two pieces
2 tablespoons *patis* (fish sauce), or more to taste
Salt and pepper to taste
1 whole medium cabbage, quartered

Patis and Calamansi Dip
125ml ($^1/_2$ cup) *patis*
Juice of 3–4 *calamansi*

1 Place chicken and onion in a casserole and pour in the water. Bring to the boil, then lower heat to medium and simmer for 20 minutes.

2 Add potatoes and, after 5 minutes, the bananas. Continue simmering until chicken, potatoes and bananas are tender, about 10 more minutes. Season with *patis*, salt and pepper.

3 Add cabbage and cook just until cabbage becomes tender-crisp, about 2 minutes.

4 To make Dip, combine *patis* and *calamansi* juice in a bowl.

5 Serve soup hot with rice and dip.

Serves 4–6
Preparation time: **5 mins**
Cooking time: **35–45 mins**

Picadillo (Ground Beef and Vegetable Soup)

2 tablespoons oil
1 small onion, chopped
3–4 cloves garlic, chopped
³/₄ kg (1¹/₂ lb) minced beef
1¹/₂ liters (6 cups) beef stock or water
1 medium potato, peeled and diced
1 small carrot, peeled and diced
50 g (1 cup) spinach leaves (optional)
2 tablespoons *patis* (fish sauce)
Salt and pepper to taste

1 Heat oil in a casserole or large saucepan and sauté onion until transparent, 1 to 2 minutes. Add garlic and sauté until fragrant, about 1 minute.

2 Stir in minced beef and cook until brown. Pour in stock or water and bring to the boil then simmer over medium heat. Add diced potatoes and carrots and simmer until potatoes and carrots are tender, about 10 minutes. Stir in spinach leaves if desired and heat through. Season with *patis*, salt and pepper.

Serves 6
Preparation time: **10 mins**
Cooking time: **20 mins**

Tinolang Manok (Ginger Chicken Soup)

2 tablespoons corn oil
3–4 cloves garlic, crushed
30 g (1 oz) ginger, peeled and sliced into rounds
1 kg (2 lb) whole chicken, cut into serving pieces
1 1/2 liters (6 cups) water
200 g (7 oz) raw papaya, peeled and cut into serving pieces
2 tablespoons *patis* (fish sauce)
1 tablespoon salt
50 g (1 1/2 cups) *malunggay* leaves, substitute with spinach or watercress

1 Heat oil in a casserole and sauté garlic for 1 minute. Add ginger and chicken and brown chicken lightly, then pour in the water.
2 Simmer chicken until almost tender, about 20 minutes. Add papaya, and season with *patis* and salt. Allow to simmer over medium heat until chicken is fully cooked and papaya is tender, about 10 more minutes.
3 Stir in *malunggay* leaves. Heat through. Serve hot with additional *patis*, if desired.

Serves 6
Preparation time: **10 mins**
Cooking time: **35 mins**

Beef Bulalo (Bone Marrow Soup)

2 kg (4 lb) beef bone marrow, have your butcher slice it

1 onion, sliced

3 liters (12 cups) water

$^3/_4$ kg (1$^1/_2$ lb) boneless beef shank or stewing beef

2–3 medium potatoes, peeled and quartered

2–3 *saba* (plantain) bananas, each cut into two pieces

1 whole medium cabbage, quartered

3–4 tablespoons *patis* (fish sauce)

Salt and pepper to taste

1 Place bone marrow and onion in a stockpot, pour in water and bring to the boil. Lower heat and simmer for about 40 minutes. Add the boneless beef shank or stewing beef. Return to the boil, then lower heat and simmer until beef is tender, about 1 to 1 $^1/_2$ hours.

2 Add the potatoes and bananas. Simmer until potatoes and bananas are tender, about 10 to 15 minutes. Add the cabbage. Stir in *patis*, salt and pepper. Cook until cabbage is tender-crisp, about 2 minutes.

3 Serve with rice and Patis and Calamansi Dip (see page 10).

Serves 6
Preparation time: **10 mins**
Cooking time: **2$^1/_2$ hours**

Pancit Bihon (Stir-fried Vermicelli)

100 g (1 cup) small prawns, peeled (heads and shells reserved)
750 ml (3 cups) water
60 ml ($^1/_4$ cup) oil
2 Chinese sausages, sliced diagonally into 1-cm ($^1/_2$-in) pieces
1 small onion, chopped
3–4 cloves garlic, chopped
200 g (1 cup) diced pork
150 g (2 cups) shredded cabbage
1 medium carrot, peeled and cut into 1-cm ($^1/_2$-in) slices
60 g (3/4 cup) sliced *Baguio* (or French) beans
60 g (2 oz) snow peas
2 chicken stock cubes
250 g (8 oz) *bihon* noodles (dried rice vermicelli), soaked in water
2 tablespoons soy sauce
1 tablespoon Hoisin sauce

1 Boil the reserved prawn heads and shells in the water for 5 minutes, then strain and discard solids. Set prawn stock aside.

2 Heat 2 tablespoons of the cooking oil in a frying pan and sauté the sausage slices until cooked. Remove from pan and set aside.

3 Heat remaining oil in a wok and sauté the onion until transparent, about 1 to 2 minutes. Add the garlic and sauté 1 minute. Brown the diced pork. Add cabbage, carrot, beans and snow peas and cook, stirring, until vegetables are almost tender.

4 Pour in the reserved prawn stock and add the chicken stock cubes. Bring to a simmer over low heat. Drain the noodles and add to the wok. When noodles are almost cooked, about 5 minutes, add the prawns and sautéed sausage slices. Blend in soy sauce and Hoisin sauce. Simmer mixture until prawns are fully cooked, about 2 to 3 minutes. Serve with *calamansi.*

Serves 4–6
Preparation time: **20 mins**
Cooking time: **20–25 mins**

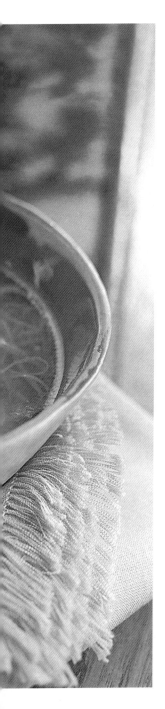

Misua with Bola Bola
(Wheat Noodles with Pork Balls)

500 g (1 lb) minced pork
1 medium carrot, peeled and chopped
$^1/_2$ medium onion, chopped
1 egg
1 tablespoon flour
Salt and pepper
2 liters (8 cups) water
2 chicken stock cubes
100 g (3$^1/_2$ oz) *misua* (wheat noodles)
2 teaspoons *patis* (fish sauce)
Chopped spring onions, to garnish (optional)

1 Combine pork, carrot, onion, egg and flour in a mixing bowl. Season with salt and pepper and mix well. Shape into meatballs and set aside.
2 In a deep saucepan or a casserole, bring water to the boil. Drop in pork balls and simmer over medium heat until balls are fully cooked, about 15 minutes.
3 Stir in stock cubes. When cubes have dissolved, add the *misua*. Season with *patis*. Simmer 2 to 3 minutes (*misua* cooks very quickly), garnish with spring onions, if desired, and serve.

Serves 6
Preparation time: **30 mins**
Cooking time: **15–20 mins**

Pancit Canton (Canton-style Noodles)

2 tablespoons oil
1 small onion, chopped
2 tablespoons finely
  chopped garlic
200 g (1 cup) diced pork
250 g (8$^1/_2$ oz) sliced
  chicken breast or thigh
1 medium carrot, peeled
  and sliced
100 g (3 oz) snow peas
150 g (2 cups) sliced
  cabbage
12 quail eggs, hard-
  boiled and peeled
250 g (8 oz) squid balls,
  fried until brown
375 ml (1$^1/_2$ cups) water
2 chicken or beef stock
  cubes
250 g (8 oz) *canton*
  (fresh egg) noodles
2 tablespoons soy sauce
3 tablespoons butter
Sliced boiled egg,
  to garnish (optional)

Calamansi Soy Dip
60 ml ($^1/_4$ cup) soy
  sauce
Juice of 2 small *calamansi*

1 Heat oil in a wok and sauté onion until transparent, about 1 to 2 minutes. Add the garlic and sauté until fragrant, about 1 minute. Add the diced pork and cook until brown. Add the chicken breast and stir-fry about 2 to 3 minutes.

2 Add carrot and, after 5 minutes, the snow peas and cabbage, quail eggs and squid balls. Stir-fry, mixing well. Pour in water and add chicken stock cubes. Simmer over medium heat about 1 minute, then add noodles and soy sauce.

3 Simmer until almost all the liquid is absorbed and canton noodles are tender, about 5 to 10 minutes. Stir in butter and mix to coat noodles with butter.

4 To make Calamansi Soy Dip, combine soy sauce and *calamansi* juice in a bowl.

5 Garnish noodles with sliced boiled egg, if desired, and serve with dip.

Serves 6
Preparation time: **30 mins**
Cooking time: **20 mins**

Morisqueta Tostada
(Prawn and Sausage Fried Rice)

This dish is typical of what is known in the Philippines as *Comida China*: Chinese dishes with Spanish names. Both the Spaniards and the Chinese were a very strong presence in the Philippines during the colonial days from the 16th to the early 20th century. When the Chinese opened the first restaurants known as *panciterias*, Spanish was the language of commerce, hence the dishes acquired Spanish names.

125 ml ($^1/_2$ cup) water
2 Chinese sausages
60 ml ($^1/_4$ cup) oil
2 eggs, lightly beaten
1 medium white or
  yellow onion, chopped
4 cloves garlic, peeled
  and crushed
250 g (8 oz) medium
  prawns, peeled
900 g (6 cups) cooked
  white rice
5 teaspoons soy sauce
3 spring onions, chopped

Serves 6
Preparation time: **5 mins**
Cooking time: **30 mins**

1 Pour the water into a frying pan and simmer the sausages over low heat until the water evaporates, about 5 to 10 minutes. Continue to fry the sausages in their own fat until fully cooked, turning frequently. Remove sausages from pan, cool a few minutes, then slice diagonally into 1-cm ($^1/_2$-in) pieces. Set aside.
2 Heat 1 tablespoon of the oil in a pan and scramble the eggs. Remove scrambled eggs from pan and cut into 1-cm ($^1/_2$-in) pieces. Set aside.
3 Heat remaining oil in a wok. Sauté onion until transparent, 1 to 2 minutes. Add garlic and sauté until fragrant. Stir in prawns and cook until almost done, about 1 to 2 minutes.
4 Immediately stir in the cooked rice, the cooked sausages and the scrambled eggs. Season with soy sauce. Stir-fry, distributing all ingredients evenly, until rice becomes a nice brown color. Garnish with spring onions.

Rellenong Talong (Stuffed Eggplant)

6 medium eggplants
  (aubergines)
2 tablespoons corn oil
1/2 medium onion,
  minced
6 cloves garlic, minced
500 g (1 lb) minced pork
2 eggs
1 teaspoon salt
60 g (1/2 cup) flour for
  dredging
125 ml (1/2 cup) corn oil
  for frying
Chopped tomato,
  to garnish (optional)
Chopped spring onion,
  to garnish (optional)

Serves 6
Preparation time: **10 mins**
Cooking time: **40 mins**

1 Grill eggplants until soft, about 10 minutes each side. Peel but do not remove stems. Flatten eggplants with the back of a fork into a fan-like shape. Set aside.
2 In a frying pan, heat corn oil for 1 minute. Sauté onion until soft, then add garlic and sauté until fragrant. Add the minced pork and cook until it turns brown and loses its raw color. Remove from heat.
3 Beat eggs in a shallow bowl. Dip the flattened eggplants in the beaten eggs. Spoon some of the cooked pork into each eggplant and season with salt. Dredge with flour so the pork will adhere to the eggplant.
4 Heat oil in a wok, then fry the eggplants one or two at a time until brown. With a heat-proof spatula turn eggplants over to brown the other side. Remove from pan and drain on paper towels.
5 If desired, garnish with tomato and spring onion and serve.

Flatten eggplants with the back of a fork into a fan-like shape.

Spoon some of the cooked pork into each eggplant.

Guisadong Repolyo (Sautéed Cabbage)

60 ml (¹/₄ cup) oil
1 small onion, chopped
Cloves of ¹/₂ head of garlic, crushed
125 g (4 oz) diced pork
250 g (8 oz) chicken liver, sliced
250 g (8 oz) chicken breast or fillet, sliced
250 g (8 oz) white cabbage, cut into 6-cm (2¹/₂-in) squares
500 ml (2 cups) water
2 chicken stock cubes
2 tablespoons soy sauce

1 Heat oil in a wok or casserole. Sauté onion until transparent, 1 to 2 minutes. Add garlic and sauté until fragrant, about 1 minute. Brown diced pork. Add chicken liver and chicken breast and sauté until almost cooked.

2 Stir in cabbage. Pour in water and add the stock cubes. Let simmer over medium heat until cabbage is crisp-tender, about 3 minutes. Season with soy sauce.

Serves 6
Preparation time: **15 mins**
Cooking time: **15–20 mins**

Mongo Guisado (Stewed Mung Beans)

1 liter (4 cups) water
250 g (1¼ cups) green *mongo* (mung) beans
2 tablespoons oil
½ small onion, chopped
3–4 cloves garlic, chopped
100 g (½ cup) diced pork
100 g (1 cup) small prawns, peeled, heads discarded
2 tablespoons *patis* (fish sauce)
Salt and pepper to taste
100 g (3½ oz) *chicharon* (pork crackers), coarsely ground

1 Soak the mung beans in about 500 ml (2 cups) water for 4 hours. Bring the same water to the boil and simmer beans until tender and most of the water has been absorbed, about 20 to 30 minutes. Set aside.
2 Heat oil in a casserole and sauté onion and garlic until soft and fragrant. Add diced pork and sauté until brown. Stir in mung beans and 500 ml (2 cups) fresh water. Bring to the boil and simmer over medium heat until pork is fully cooked (add more water if necessary). Add the prawns and cook until they turn orange in color, about 1 to 2 minutes. Season with *patis*, salt and pepper.
3 Add the *chicharon*. Heat through; pour into serving bowls, and serve with rice.

Serves 6
Preparation time: **10 minutes + 4 hours soaking**
Cooking time: **30–40 mins**

Place lettuce leaf on a wrapper and add ubod filling and spring onion.

Roll up the wrapper to enclose the filling ingredients.

Lumpiang Ubod
(Spring Roll with Heart of Palm)

500 g (1 lb) *ubod*
(heart of palm)
1 liter (4 cups) water
2 tablespoons oil
1 small onion, minced
3–4 cloves garlic, minced
200 g (1 cup) diced pork
100 g (1 cup) small
prawns, peeled
1 tablespoon *patis* (fish
sauce)
60 ml ($1/4$ cup) Brown
Sauce (see recipe
below)
Lumpia Spring Roll
Wrappers (see recipe
below) or bought
12–14 lettuce leaves
12–14 spring onions
(white part only)
Cloves of $1/2$ head of
garlic, crushed

Brown Sauce
150 g (1 cup) brown
sugar
500 ml (2 cups) water
1 teaspoon salt
2 tablespoons soy sauce
2 tablespoons cornflour
dissolved in 60 ml
($1/4$ cup) water

Spring Roll Wrappers
1 egg
125 g (1 cup) plain (all-
purpose) flour
375 ml ($1 1/2$ cups) water
$1/2$ teaspoon salt
1 teaspoon oil

1 To make the Brown Sauce, combine sugar, water, salt and soy sauce in a saucepan. Bring to the boil, then simmer for about 5 minutes. Stir dissolved corn-flour into the saucepan and simmer until mixture thickens, about 10 to 15 minutes. Set aside.

2 To make the Spring Roll Wrappers, beat egg in a mixing bowl until thick. Blend in flour and water alternately, beating with a wire whisk until mixture is smooth. Add salt. The batter should be thin and pourable. Heat a non-stick frying pan and brush very lightly with the oil. Pour about $1/4$ cup of the batter into the hot pan and tilt the pan immediately to swirl the batter so it is spread evenly across the pan. Cook the batter until it solidifies, about 45 seconds to 1 minute. Run a metal spatula around the edges of the pan to loosen the cooked egg wrapper. Flip pan onto a plate to release the wrapper. Repeat with remaining batter, brushing pan with oil only if necessary. Be careful not to tear the wrappers. Makes 12 to 14 wrappers.

3 To make filling, cut open *ubod* and julienne the *ubod* meat. Boil in the water until tender but still firm, about 10 minutes. Drain. In a wok, heat oil and sauté onion and garlic about 1 minute. Add the diced pork and cook until brown. Stir in prawns and the drained *ubod*. Continue stirring until prawns are cooked. Season with *patis* and blend in 60 ml ($1/4$ cup) brown sauce. Stir well to mix, then cool a few minutes.

4 To assemble, line each spring roll wrapper with a lettuce leaf. Spoon 1 to 2 tablespoons of the *ubod* filling into the wrapper and add the spring onion. Roll the wrapper to enclose the filling. Pour brown sauce over the wrapper and top with crushed garlic.

Serves 6–7
Preparation time: **30 mins**
Cooking time: **30–40 mins**

Adobong Kangkong
(Kangkong Cooked in Vinegar and Soy Sauce)

The vinegar and soy sauce combination gives this dish a piquant flavor. The perfect accompaniment for it is a bowl of steaming hot white rice.

200 g (7 oz) *kangkong* (water convolvulus)
60 ml (¹/₄ cup) cane or white vinegar
2 tablespoons soy sauce
60 ml (¹/₄ cup) water
1 tablespoon oyster sauce
1 tablespoon oil
100 g (¹/₂ cup) diced pork
¹/₂ onion, chopped
3 cloves garlic, crushed

Serves 4
Preparation time: **5 mins**
Cooking time: **10 mins**

1 Trim the *kangkong*, separating the leaves from the stalks. Set aside both leaves and stalks. In a small bowl combine vinegar, soy sauce, water and oyster sauce.
2 In a frying pan, heat oil over medium heat. Add diced pork and sauté 2 minutes.
3 Push the pork to one side of pan. Add the onion and garlic and sauté about 1 minute. Add *kangkong* stalks and stir-fry 2 minutes, then add the leaves. Pour in the vinegar and soy sauce mixture.
4 Cover pan and let simmer until stalks and leaves are tender but still crisp, 1 to 2 minutes. Serve immediately with rice.

Red Egg Salad

A traditional Filipino delicacy, red eggs are made from duck eggs which are buried in salt for several weeks to make them salty. They get their name from the color of the shells, which are dyed red, perhaps to distinguish them from other types of egg. The best red eggs are said to be from Pateros, a town known for its duck raising industry. In this salad, the saltiness of the red eggs is balanced by the eggplants, tomatoes and onion.

200 g (3 medium) eggplants (aubergines)
6 red eggs (salty eggs)
6 medium tomatoes, coarsely chopped
1 small onion, finely chopped
Juice of 1 *calamansi* (optional)
1 tablespoon *patis* (fish sauce) (optional)

1 Grill the eggplants about 10 minutes on each side or until soft. Peel and slice into 2-cm (1-in) pieces.
2 Peel eggs and slice into 2-cm (1-in) pieces.
3 Toss together eggplants, eggs, tomatoes and onion in a salad bowl. Season with juice of *calamansi* and *patis* if desired.
4 Serve with rice and fried fish, Tapa or Tocino.

Serves 6
Preparation time: **25 mins**
Cooking time: **20 mins**

Camaron Rebosado
(Battered Prawns in Sweet & Sour Sauce)

250 g (2 cups) plain (all-purpose) flour
2 teaspoons salt
1 kg (2 lb) medium prawns, heads and shells removed,
   deveined, tails left intact
2 large eggs, lightly beaten
250 ml (1 cup) oil

Sweet and Sour Sauce
100 g ($^1/_2$ cup) white refined sugar
$^1/_2$ teaspoon salt
60 ml ($^1/_4$ cup) tomato ketchup
125 ml ($^1/_2$ cup) vinegar
2 tablespoons cornflour dissolved in 250 ml (1 cup)
   water

1 In a mixing bowl, combine flour and salt. Dredge
each prawn in flour mixture, dip in egg, then dredge
in flour again.
2 Heat cooking oil in a wok or frying pan. Cook prawns
in hot oil in batches until they turn an even yellow-
orange color. Drain on paper towels.
3 To make the Sweet and Sour Sauce, blend sugar, salt,
ketchup and vinegar in a saucepan. Bring to a simmer
over low heat. Stir in the cornflour mixture.
4 Continue simmering until sauce is thick, stirring
occasionally. Pour over cooked prawns or serve as a
side dip.

Serves 6
Preparation time: **40 mins**
Cooking time: **40 mins–1 hour**

Paksiw na Tiyan ng Bangus
(Milkfish Belly Stewed in Vinegar)

Bangus belly is prized for its black, fatty layer, which has a very soft texture. The vinegar stew and ginger give this prime cut a piquant, slightly sour flavor.

1 small *ampalaya* (bitter melon), about 100 g (3$^1/_3$ oz), sliced about 1 cm ($^1/_2$ in) thick
2 small eggplants (aubergines), about 100 g (3$^1/_3$ oz), sliced diagonally about 1 cm ($^1/_2$ in) thick
6 fillets *bangus* (milkfish) belly
250 ml (1 cup) vinegar
125 ml ($^1/_2$ cup) water
2 tablespoons sliced ginger
1 green chili (optional)
Salt and pepper to taste

1 In a non-metallic or enamel pan, layer the *ampalaya*, eggplants and *bangus* fillets. Mix together vinegar and water and pour into pan. Add the sliced ginger and chili, if desired, and season with salt and pepper.
2 Cover pan and allow mixture to simmer until fish fillets are fully cooked, about 15 minutes. Serve with rice.

Serves 4–6
Preparation time: **5 mins**
Cooking time: **15 mins**

Ampalaya, also known as bitter melon, is a cylindrical, wrinkled, green "melon" which has a distinctive bitter taste. It is available from Filipino grocers.

Inihaw na Bangus (Grilled Stuffed Milkfish)

1 *bangus* (milkfish),
about 600 g (1lb 3 oz)
Salt and pepper to taste
3–4 medium tomatoes,
chopped
1 large onion, chopped

Serves 2–4
Preparation time: **30 mins**
Cooking time: **40 mins**

1 Clean *bangus* well and slit open down the length (from head to tail). For easier dining, remove all the bones. Season with salt and pepper.

2 Combine tomatoes and onion in a bowl. Season with salt and pepper. Spoon into the *bangus*, stuffing the entire cavity of the fish. (Reserve any excess stuffing and serve separately with the fish.) Close the fish and wrap tightly in aluminum foil.

3 Grill or broil fish until fully cooked, about 20 minutes on each side. Serve with rice and Calamansi Soy Dip (see page 18) .

Fish Sarciado (Fried Fish Steaks)

The mixture of garlic, onions and tomatoes enhances the flavor of the sautéed fish. The olive oil gives it a Mediterranean touch.

4 *tanguinge* (Spanish mackerel) steaks
Juice of 4 *calamansi*
125 ml ($^1/_2$ cup) olive oil
Cloves of $^1/_2$ head garlic, crushed
1 large onion, chopped
1 medium tomato, chopped
2 tablespoons *patis* (fish sauce)
250 ml (1 cup) water

Serves 4
Preparation time: **5 mins**
 + 30 mins marinating
Cooking time: **15 mins**

1 Marinate fish steaks in *calamansi* juice for about 30 minutes. In a frying pan, heat about 90 ml ($^1/_3$ cup) of the olive oil and sauté the fish steaks until fully cooked, about 6 minutes on the first side and 5 minutes on the other side. Remove fish steaks from frying pan and set aside.

2 In another pan, heat remaining oil and sauté garlic, onion and tomatoes, until tender but not limp. Stir in *patis* and water. Simmer until most of the liquid has been absorbed.

3 Spoon onion and tomato mixture over the cooked fish steaks. Serve with rice.

Daing na Bangus
(Milkfish Marinated in Vinegar and Garlic)

1 whole *bangus* (milk-fish), about 600 g (1 lb 3 oz), deboned
Cloves of 1 whole head of garlic, crushed
180 ml ($^3/_4$ cup) vinegar
Freshly ground pepper
1 teaspoon salt
60 ml ($^1/_4$ cup) oil
Spring onions, to garnish (optional)

Garlic-Vinegar Dip
250 ml (1 cup) vinegar
Cloves of $^1/_2$ head garlic, crushed
Freshly ground pepper, to taste

1 Flatten *bangus* on its back (it is usually sold like this when deboned) and place in a marinating pan. Sprinkle garlic all over fish, pour in vinegar and season with pepper and salt. Cover and leave in the refrigerator for several hours or overnight.

2 When ready to cook, heat oil in a large wok. Fry *bangus* until fully cooked, about 6 to 7 minutes on the first side and 5 minutes on the second side.

3 To make dip, combine vinegar, garlic and pepper in a bowl. Let stand a few minutes before serving.

4 Remove bangus to serving platter and garnish with spring onions, if desired.

5 Serve with rice and Garlic-Vinegar Dip.

Serves 4
Preparation time: **5 mins + overnight marinating**
Cooking time: **15 mins**

Adobong Pusit
(Squid Cooked in Vinegar)

Squid cooks very quickly so make sure you watch the pan during the cooking process. Serve this dish with hot, steaming rice.

1 kg (2 lb) small squid
2 tablespoons oil
Cloves of $1/2$ head garlic, crushed
125 ml ($1/2$ cup) vinegar
60 ml ($1/4$ cup) water
$1/2$ teaspoon salt

1 Press on the heads of the squids to remove all the black ink (and reserve all the ink). Remove the membranes, heads and tentacles from squid. Discard membranes and heads but retain the tentacles.
2 In a frying pan, heat oil and brown the garlic. Remove garlic and set aside.
3 In a non-metallic saucepan, combine squid, tentacles, vinegar, water and reserved ink. Simmer over medium heat until squid are cooked, about 2 minutes. Do not overcook or the squid will become tough.Season with salt.
4 Remove from heat. Sprinkle fried garlic on top and serve immediately with rice.

Serves 4
Preparation time: **15 mins**
Cooking time: **5 mins**

Fritada
(Chicken in Tomato Sauce)

60 ml ($^1/_4$ cup) olive oil
1 small onion, chopped
3–4 cloves garlic, crushed
1 whole chicken, about 1 kg (2 lb), cut into
    serving pieces
250 g (1 cup) crushed canned tomatoes
250 ml (1 cup) water
1 bay leaf
2–3 medium potatoes, peeled, quartered and fried
1 red or green capsicum, cut in 1-cm ($^1/_2$-in) strips
85 g ($^2/_3$ cup) pitted green (or other) olives
200 g (1$^1/_2$ cups) frozen green peas, thawed
Salt and pepper

1 Heat olive oil in a casserole. Sauté onion until
transparent, then add garlic and sauté until fragrant.
Brown the chicken pieces on all sides. Pour in crushed
tomatoes and water. Add the bay leaf, bring to the
boil, then simmer until chicken is almost tender,
about 20 minutes.
2 Add the fried potatoes, capsicum strips and olives
and simmer until chicken is tender, 5 to 10 more
minutes. Stir in green peas and season with salt and
pepper. Remove the bay leaf before serving.

Serves 6
Preparation time: **15 mins**
Cooking time: **30–40 mins**

Menudo
(Diced Pork in Tomato Sauce)

This easy-to-prepare dish is ideal for a weekday dinner. The pork, potatoes and carrots all cook very quickly, and the tomato sauce adds valuable nutrients, such as lycopene, to the dish.

2 tablespoons oil
1 small onion, chopped
1 tablespoon chopped garlic
1 kg (2 lb) pork shoulder, cut into 1-cm ($^1/_2$-in) pieces
1 large potato, cubed
2 medium carrots, cubed
250 ml (1 cup) water
500 ml (2 cups) canned tomato sauce
2 tablespoons soy sauce or to taste
2 tablespoons *calamansi* juice

1 Heat cooking oil in a large frying pan or wok and sauté onion about 1 minute. Add garlic and sauté a further 1 minute.
2 Add pork and stir to brown the pork pieces evenly. Add cubed potatoes and carrots and stir to mix.
3 Pour in water and simmer for about 15 minutes. Blend in tomato sauce, soy sauce and *calamansi* juice. Stir to combine mixture well.
4 Bring to the boil, then immediately lower heat. Let simmer until pork is thoroughly cooked and potatoes and carrots are tender, about 15 minutes.
5 Serve warm with rice or bread.

Serves 6
Preparation time: **10 mins**
Cooking time: **35 mins**

Cut wrapper into two. Spoon 2 tablespoons of ground pork mixture into each wrapper.

Moisten edges of wrapper with egg and water mixture. Roll wrapper and seal the edges.

44

Lumpiang Shanghai (Fried Pork Spring Rolls)

3 tablespoons corn oil
3–4 cloves garlic,
  chopped
1 medium onion,
  chopped
750 g (1 1/2 lb) minced
  pork
250 g (8 oz) small
  prawns, peeled and
  coarsely diced
1/4 cup chopped spring
  onions
1/2 cup diced *singkamas*
  (jicama)
1 medium carrot,
  chopped
Salt and pepper
1 large egg
1–2 tablespoons water
30 pieces *lumpia* (spring
  roll wrappers)
500 ml (2 cups) corn oil
  for frying
Sweet and Sour Sauce
  (see page 30)

1 Heat oil in a frying-pan and sauté garlic and onion. Add pork and brown lightly. Add the prawns, spring onions, *jicama* and carrot and sauté until pork is thoroughly cooked, stirring to mix well. Season with salt and pepper. Let mixture cool.

2 Combine egg and water in a small bowl. Cut each *lumpia* wrapper in two. Spoon about 2 tablespoons of ground pork mixture onto each wrapper. Moisten edges of wrapper with egg and water mixture. Roll wrapper and seal the edges.

3 Heat half of the corn oil in a frying-pan. Fry the rolled wrappers in the hot oil until brown. Add more oil if necessary and fry the remaining *lumpia*. Serve with Sweet and Sour Sauce (see page 30).

Serves 6–8
Preparation time: **30 mins**
Cooking time: **40 mins**

Bistek Tagalog (Sirloin Steak Filipino-style)

500 g (1 lb) beef sirloin, thinly sliced
Juice of 12 *calamansi*
60 ml ($^1/_4$ cup) cooking oil
1 medium onion, sliced into rings
60 ml ($^1/_4$ cup) soy sauce
125 ml ($^1/_2$ cup) water
2–3 potatoes, peeled, cut into wedges and fried

Serves 4
Preparation time: **5 mins**
  + **30 mins marinating**
Cooking time: **15 mins**

1 Marinate beef in half of the *calamansi* juice for about 30 minutes.

2 Heat oil in a frying pan and sauté onion rings until lightly brown. Remove onions from frying pan and set aside.

3 Drain beef slices from marinade and reserve marinade. Sauté beef in the same frying pan 1 to 2 minutes, then turn to cook other side for 1 to 2 minutes.

4 Combine remaining *calamansi* juice, soy sauce and water. Stir into frying-pan together with reserved marinade.

5 Return onion to pan and simmer about 1 to 2 minutes. Serve with fried potato wedges and rice.

Inihaw na Baboy
(Grilled Marinated Pork)

1 kg (2 lb) pork belly
Cloves of 1 head of garlic, crushed
125 ml ($^1/_2$ cup) 7-Up or Sprite
125 ml ($^1/_2$ cup) vinegar
2 tablespoons sugar
Freshly ground black pepper

Vinegar-Soy Dip
1 medium onion, finely diced
250 ml (1 cup) vinegar
125 ml ($^1/_2$ cup) soy sauce
Freshly ground pepper
1 sliced finger chili, (optional)

1 Slice pork belly lengthwise about 2 cm ($^3/_4$ in) wide.
2 Combine garlic, Sprite or 7-Up, vinegar, sugar and pepper in a bowl. Pour over pork belly. Cover and marinate 3 to 4 hours in refrigerator.
3 When ready to cook, drain pork and discard marinade. Heat grill to medium and grill pork until thoroughly cooked, about 15 to 20 minutes on the first side and 10 minutes on the second side.
4 To make the Vinegar-Soy Dip, combine the onion, vinegar, soy sauce and pepper in a bowl. Stir to blend. For a spicier dip, add the sliced chili, if desired.
5 Serve the grilled pork with the dip and cooked white rice.

Makes 4 to 6 Servings
Preparation time: 5 mins + at least 1 hour for marination
Cooking time: 30 mins

Chicken and Pork Adobo

1 kg (2 lbs) pork belly or shoulder, cut into large chunks
1 whole chicken, cut into serving pieces
1 head of garlic, cloves crushed
375 ml (1^1/$_2$ cups) vinegar
375 ml (1^1/$_2$ cups) water
1 bay leaf (optional)
2 tablespoons coarse salt
125 ml (^{1}/$_2$ cup) oil
60 ml (^{1}/$_4$ cup) soy sauce

Serves 8–10
Preparation time: **10 mins**
Cooking time: **1 hour**

1 Put pork belly and chicken in a large casserole dish. Sprinkle garlic over pork and chicken. Combine vinegar and water and pour into casserole. Do not use an aluminum casserole dish as the aluminum will react to the vinegar.

2 Bring to a boil without stirring. When mixture boils, lower heat to simmer and add bay leaf, if using. Add salt and allow to simmer until meats are tender, about 30 minutes. Remove from casserole, reserving any liquid.

3 In a wok, heat oil and brown the pork and chicken in batches. Remove from oil as pork and chicken brown and arrange in a serving dish.

4 Blend together soy sauce and reserved liquid. Pour over chicken and pork. Serve with hot rice and chopped tomatoes.

Beef Tapa (Cured Beef)

110 g (³/₄ cup) brown
 sugar
2 tablespoons garlic salt,
 substitute with 1 table-
 spoon salt and 4 cloves
 garlic, minced
125 ml (¹/₂ cup) vinegar
500 g (1 lb) sirloin beef,
 thinly sliced into serving
 pieces
125 ml (¹/₂ cup) oil

Serves 4–6
Preparation time: **10 mins
 + overnight marinating**
Cooking time: **15–20 mins**

1 Combine sugar, garlic salt and vinegar in a mixing
bowl. Coat each piece of beef in the mixture, making
sure to coat all sides well. Arrange beef in a marinating
pan. Pour any extra marinade over beef. Refrigerate
for a few hours or overnight.

2 When ready to cook, heat 2 tablespoons of the oil in
a frying pan. Fry beef slices in batches, just until
cooked through. Add more oil whenever necessary to
finish frying all the beef slices.

3 Drain beef on paper towels. Serve with rice topped
with fried egg and sliced tomatoes or Garlic-Vinegar
Dip (see page 36).

Estofado (Stewed Pork)

150 g ($^3/_4$ cup) sugar
250 ml (1 cup) vinegar
125 ml (1/2 cup) dark soy sauce
250 ml (1 cup) water
60 ml ($^1/_4$ cup) corn oil
Cloves of 1 head garlic, crushed
1 kg (2 lb) boneless pork shoulder, cut into large cubes
1 bay leaf
1 medium carrot, sliced into 1-cm ($^1/_2$-in) rounds
3–4 *saba* (plantain) bananas, sliced diagonally into
  5-cm (2-in) pieces
4 *pan de sal* (Filipino buns), each cut into four pieces
  (optional)
Spring onion, to garnish (optional)

1 Combine sugar, vinegar, soy sauce and water in a
mixing bowl. Set aside to allow flavors to blend.
2 Heat 2 tablespoons of the oil in a casserole. Fry the
garlic until brown. Remove garlic from pan and set aside.
3 Pour in remaining oil and heat. Add pork and
brown lightly on all sides. Pour in vinegar mixture.
Bring to the boil, then lower heat to simmer. (Do not
stir, or the vinegar will have a "raw" taste). Add bay leaf
and simmer for about 20 minutes or until pork is
almost tender.
4 Add the carrot and, 5 minutes later, the bananas.
When bananas and carrot are almost tender, about
5 minutes more, stir in *pan de sal*. Continue simmering
until pork is fully cooked and bananas and carrot are
completely tender, about 5 minutes. Garnish with
spring onion, if desired.
5 Serve with rice or additional *pan de sal*.

Serves 6
Preparation time: 5–10 mins
Cooking time: 45 mins

Longganisa (Filipino Sausage)

500 g (1 lb) minced pork
200 g (1 cup) diced pork fat
3 tablespoons brown sugar
2 teaspoons salt
Freshly ground black pepper
2 tablespoons finely chopped garlic
2 tablespoons crushed garlic
1 tablespoon annatto seeds
60 ml ($^1/_4$ cup) vinegar
60–125 ml ($^1/_4$ to $^1/_2$ cup) oil
Spring onion, to garnish (optional)

1 In a mixing bowl, combine minced pork, pork fat, sugar, salt, pepper and garlic. In a small bowl, combine annatto seeds and vinegar. Press on the annatto seeds with the back of a spoon to extract the color. Strain vinegar into the pork mixture. Mix well by hand or with a wooden spoon.
2 Shape into 8 $^1/_2$-cm (4-in) sausages and roll in small pieces of wax paper. Chill for a few hours in the refrigerator.
3 When ready to cook, heat oil in a wok or frying-pan. Unwrap the sausages and fry in batches in hot oil until fully cooked. Drain on paper towels.
4 Garnish with spring onion, if desired, and serve with rice and tomatoes or Garlic-Vinegar Dip (see page 36). These sausages can also be frozen until needed.

Annatto seeds are known as *atsuete* in Tagalog. These dried, dark reddish-brown seeds are often used as food coloring or dye. The seeds are soaked, then squeezed in water to extract the red coloring, which lends an orange to reddish tint to food.

Makes 18–20 sausages
Preparation time: 30 mins + 2 hours chilling
Cooking time: 30 mins

Pork Tocino (Cured Pork)

110 g (³/₄ cup) brown
  sugar
250 ml (1 cup) canned
  pineapple juice
Freshly ground pepper
500 g (1 lb) pork shoulder,
  thinly sliced
125 ml (¹/₂ cup) oil
Spring onion, to garnish
  (optional)

Serves 4–6
Preparation time: **10 mins**
  + overnight marinating
Cooking time: **20–25 mins**

1 Combine sugar, pineapple juice and ground pepper in a bowl to make marinade. Dip each slice of pork in the marinade to cover all surfaces of the meat.
2 Arrange meat in a marinating pan. Pour any extra marinade onto meat. Cover and marinate in refrigerator a few hours or overnight.
3 When ready to cook, heat half of the oil. Drain pork slices and cook in hot oil in batches, adding more oil if necessary.
4 Garnish with spring onion, if desired, and serve with rice and sliced tomatoes.

Lechon Kawali (Deep-fried Pork)

1 kg (2 lb) pork belly with skin, whole
1 whole onion, sliced
2 liters (8 cups) water for boiling
Oil for deep-frying
Water for sprinkling
Garlic Vinegar Dip

Serves 6–8
Preparation time: **5 mins**
Cooking time: **1 hour**

1 Place pork belly and onion in a stockpot, add water to cover, bring to the boil, then lower heat to medium and simmer for about 45 minutes or until pork is just tender. (Not too soft or it won't be crisp when fried). Drain pork. Pat with paper towels until very dry.

2 Heat oil in a large wok or frying pan until very hot. Carefully put pork belly in the hot oil, skin side down. The oil will spatter so be sure to have a cover handy. Cover pan; reduce heat to medium. Cook pork until skin is almost brown, about 10 minutes.

3 Turn pork over, so skin is up. Brown other side of pork , about 10 minutes. Sprinkle some water on the skin of the pork. This will make blisters form on the pork skin and make it crispy. Turn pork over so skin is down again. Continue cooking until skin is golden brown, 5 to 10 minutes. Remove from pan and drain on paper towels. Slice and serve with Garlic-Vinegar Dip (see page 36).

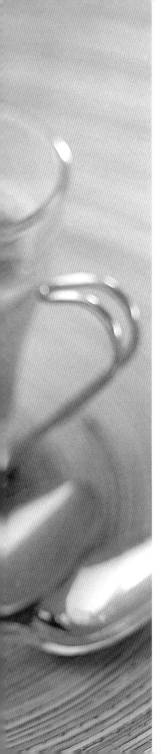

Guinataan
(Mixed Fruits Cooked in Coconut Milk and Sugar)

2 liters (8 cups) water
500 g (1 lb) sweet potatoes, peeled and cut into chunks
300 g (10 oz) taro, peeled and cut into chunks
500 g (1 lb) *ube* (purple yam), peeled and cut into chunks
6 *saba* (plantain) bananas, sliced 2 cm (1 in) thick
250 g (8 oz) *galapong* (rice flour)
250 g (8 oz) sago (tapioca pearls)
200 g ($6^2/_3$ oz) jackfruit strips
500 ml (2 cups) fresh or canned coconut cream
500 g ($2^1/_2$ cups) white refined sugar

1 Boil the water in a stockpot. Add the sweet potatoes and taro and simmer for about 5 minutes. Add the *ube* and *saba* bananas and continue simmering for a few more minutes.
2 Meanwhile roll the *galapong* into small balls. Drop the *galapong* balls, sago and jackfruit into the liquid and continue to simmer. Stir in coconut cream and sugar.
3 Simmer until all the ingredients are tender, about 20 minutes. When cooked, do not cover the pot or the mixture will spoil. Serve warm.

Serves 10–12
Preparation time: **40 mins**
Cooking time: **30 mins**

Buko Salad (Fresh Coconut Delight)

This refreshing dessert combines fresh coconut strips with canned fruits. A sweet, creamy concoction, buko salad is a favorite at Filipino gatherings.

2 cups fresh coconut meat strips
450-g (15-oz) can tropical fruit cocktail, drained
250 ml (1 cup) whipped cream
250 ml (1 cup) sweetened condensed milk

1 Toss coconut strips with drained fruit cocktail.
2 Blend whipped cream and condensed milk into the fruits and mix well.
3 Chill for several hours before serving.

Serves 8–10
Preparation time: **30 mins**

Mais Con Hielo (Milky Corn Surprise)

Part of the fun of eating this milky dessert from a parfait glass is stabbing at the crushed ice to get to the bottom of the glass, where all the sweet corn lies. A truly refreshing sweet, this is a favourite of Filipinos during the hot summer months.

2 415-g cans (30 oz) cream-style corn
150 g (3/4 cup) white refined sugar
750 ml (3 cups) evaporated or fresh milk
Crushed ice

1 You will need six dessert bowls or tall parfait glasses. Into each bowl, spoon 1/2 cup cream-style corn. Add about 2 tablespoons sugar.
2 Pour 1/2 cup milk into each bowl. Top each bowl with crushed ice.

Serves 6
Preparation time: **5 mins**

Brazo de Mercedes
(Rolled Meringue with Egg Yolk Filling)

Filling

8 egg yolks

300 ml (1¼ cups) condensed milk

2 tablespoons butter

1 tablespoon white, refined sugar

Zest of 1 lemon

Meringue

8 egg whites

1 teaspoon cream of tartar

250 g (1¼ cups) white refined sugar

1 teaspoon almond extract (optional)

¼–½ cup icing (confectioners') sugar

Serves 8–10

Preparation time: **50 mins**

Cooking time: **10 mins**

1 To make the Filling, mix egg yolks and condensed milk in a double boiler. Simmer, stirring constantly until almost thick, about 20 minutes. Add the butter and sugar and continue stirring for 5 more minutes.

2 Fold lemon zest into the mixture. Continue stirring over simmering water until orange in color and thick, about 5 to 10 more minutes. Remove from heat and set aside.

3 To make the Meringue, beat egg whites and cream of tartar in large bowl of an electric mixer until soft peaks start to form. Gradually add the sugar and almond extract, if desired, and continue beating until stiff peaks form, about 10 minutes. Do not overbeat.

4 Preheat oven to 190°C (375°F). Line a greased baking tray with waxed paper and grease waxed paper well. Sprinkle icing sugar on greased waxed paper. Spread the egg white mixture on the paper, covering it entirely. Bake until top is brown, about 10 minutes.

5 Have another greased baking tray ready. Line with greased waxed paper as before. Invert the egg white meringue onto this waxed paper so that brown side is below.

6 Spread egg yolk filling on the egg white meringue. Fold one side of the meringue towards the middle , then fold other side over to enclose filling completely. Dust with icing sugar.

Grease waxed paper on greased baking tray.

Spread the egg white mixture on top of the icing sugar on baking tray.

Remove meringue from tray and place brown side down on second greased baking tray.

Fold one side of meringue towards the middle, then the other to overlap.

Index